essentials

essentials provide up-to-date knowledge in a concentrated form. The essence of what matters as "state of the art" in the current professional discussion or in practice. essentials inform quickly, uncomplicatedly and comprehensibly

• as an introduction to a current topic from your field of expertise
• as an introduction to a subject area that is still unknown to you
• as an insight, in order to be able to speak on the subject

The books in electronic and printed form present the expert knowledge of Springer specialist authors in a compact form. They are particularly suitable for use as eBooks on tablet PCs, eBook readers and smartphones. essentials: Knowledge modules from economics, social sciences and the humanities, from technology and the natural sciences, as well as from medicine, psychology and the health professions. From renowned authors of all Springer publishing brands.

Monika Huber

Resilience In The Team

Ideas And Application Concepts For Team Development

 Springer

Monika Huber
Walk the Change
Mannheim, Germany

ISSN 2731-3107   ISSN 2731-3115   (electronic)
essentials
ISBN 978-3-658-39781-4   ISBN 978-3-658-39782-1   (eBook)
https://doi.org/10.1007/978-3-658-39782-1

This Springer imprint is published by the registered company Springer Fachmedien Wiesbaden GmbH, part of Springer Nature.
The registered company address is: Abraham-Lincoln-Str. 46, 65189 Wiesbaden, Germany

A thank you to my parents and my father.

Acknowledgements

My personal metaphor for resilience is the Japanese Kintsugi process: In this process, a broken ceramic is puttied or repaired with gold and put back together. This significantly increases the value of the ceramic. Transferred to resilience, we increase our value after a break in the currency "self-efficacy".

In my personal gain in resilience, I would like to thank many people who have supported me on my way – knowingly or unknowingly. But my special thanks go to the following:

Helga Wethje, for her unwavering optimism
Thomas Huber, for his shown resilience getting back to life
Gerhard Brunner, for his way of celebrating life
You are an inspiration to me.

And also a big thank you to my network of relationships:
Claudia Schnell, Helga Reile, Manuela Vetterli, Carolin Best, Achim Donsbach, Jana Flommersfeld, Markus Dosch, Robert Fandert, Guido Dietrich, Petra Huber and many more.

Mannheim, Germany   Monika Huber
15.10.2018

What You Can Find in This *Essential*

- Basic studies on the concept of resilience
- An extension of the resilience concept to teams
- Supporting neuroscientific findings
- Application of the resilience factors to teams

Contents

Resilience: An Introduction

1

Fall down seven times, stand up eight.

Japanese proverb

In a working environment in which the work density and thus the workload at the workplace is increasing more and more, it is all the more important to remain stress-resistant and in balance. Up to now, concepts of stress balance have been used for this purpose, but these only pick up at the point when initial stress behaviour is already present.

This contrasts with the concept of resilience, which on the one hand assumes that an adversity must first be overcome in order to demonstrate resilience, and on the other hand is understood in the sense of a preventive measure when it comes to building up resources. It follows that resilience can be trained – by strengthening personal resources and psychological resilience. Most often, these concepts are applied to individuals. But many of the insights from resilience research can be applied and even extended to teams: For example, making the team aware of its resources promotes resilience in the team, which also promotes self-efficacy. In addition, development is promoted as a side effect.

The focus of this book is on how the concept of resilience and the so-called resilience factors can be applied to teams. Aspects concerning resilient leadership or general aspects of team development are disregarded in this book, as these would go beyond the scope of what is possible in a concise overview of this specific topic.

© The Author(s), under exclusive license to Springer Fachmedien Wiesbaden GmbH, part of Springer Nature 2023
M. Huber, *Resilience In The Team*, essentials,
https://doi.org/10.1007/978-3-658-39782-1_1

The target audience for this book is team developers, coaches and interested leaders who want to deal with the topic of resilience and its promotion in the team and are looking for pragmatic approaches and solutions to it.

Resilience Research and Selected Studies on Resilience

Nothing is as practical as a good theory.

Kurt Lewin

Resilience research is a very young discipline and has its roots in developmental psychopathology, which was primarily concerned with the influences of risk on children's development in the 1970s. In the corresponding studies, it was noticed that some children had developed well despite adverse circumstances and the corresponding risks; this laid the foundation for resilience research. In addition, there were other studies that focused on "maintaining healthiness" – and thus influenced the previous pathological approach. These two studies, which are repeatedly mentioned in the current literature on resilience, have become particularly well-known:

- Emmy Werner's Kauai Study
- Aaron Antonovsky's study of salutogenesis

For this reason, a brief outline of the two studies and their significance in the context of resilience research is given below. This is followed by the introduction of selected findings from neuroscience that are helpful for understanding resilience theory. This lays the foundation for the definition of resilience.

2.1   Emmy Werner's Kauai Study

A long-term study of over 40 years, conducted by Emmy Werner on the Hawaiian island of Kauai with 698 people, followed the 1955 birth cohort prenatally, after birth, during childhood and into mature adulthood. As it is common with studies, a thesis was stated. In this case, the thesis was that children in adverse circumstances develop worse, as expected, than those without these experiences made. But the surprising thing about the result was that about a third of the children had developed quite normally – despite the adversities. These children were subsequently described as resilient. It should be noted, however, that it was not always the same group of children throughout the time frame, but that it was different children or individuals who had shown resilience at different times when the subjects were on site for examination or interview. Based on these changes, the conclusion was drawn that resilience can be acquired in the course of life – and is not – as previously thought – innate.

Emmy Werner was interested in the biological and psychosocial risk factors, as well as the stressful events and protective factors that influenced development. With the help of this study, it was possible to identify and derive various factors that are helpful for positive development in the sense of resilience. To this end, Werner identified three different levels from which the so-called protective factors originate (the opposite of protective factors are risk factors), which can interact and reinforce each other. Here is a selection of them:

1. Protective factors from the child itself: For example, among other factors, the children usually had a pleasant temperament, which caused less stress on the part of the environment.
2. Protective factors within the family: The children usually had at least one caregiver within the family with whom a close relationship or bond could be established.
3. Protective factors outside the family: The resilient children usually had a close friend outside the family or perceived their teachers as role models.

These protective factors, which were identified for the first time at that time, were repeatedly underpinned with further studies, such as the Mannheim Risk Children Study by Manfred Laucht and colleagues, which followed children born between 1986 and 1988, from the third month until the age of 11. The scientific contribution of this study is thus immense, because even from today's perspective, some conclusions from this study still form the basis for the current resilience concept. The following findings are presented in this context:

- During the long-term study on Kauai, it was found that it was not always the same group of people who were found to develop resilience. Rather, they were at different stages of life: For example, some were resilient in adulthood, while others in the group were so in childhood. This finding allows the conclusion that resilience is not inherited, but can be learned as part of a developmental process.
- The protective factors identified in the Werner study have since been further developed and are reflected in the resilience factors. The latter form an important basis when it comes to learning resilience: If, for example, a caregiver has been identified as a protective factor during development, this is reflected in the resilience factor "Shaping networks and relationships".

2.2 Aaron Antonovsky's Study on Salutogenesis

Another study that is still considered groundbreaking today for the initiation of resilience research is that of the medical sociologist Aaron Antonovsky. Under the term salutogenesis, he brought about a paradigm shift that is unparalleled: instead of concentrating on the previously common pathological approach, in which the causes of illnesses are usually investigated, Antonovsky shifted the focus of investigation to the beneficial resources of people and to the question of what ultimately helps people to overcome difficult conditions and remain healthy. Thus, as a new neologism, the term salutogenesis was coined, which can be translated as "health emergence" ("salus" means health and healing and "generare" create and generate in Latin).

For the study, which was conducted in the 1970s, women in Israel of different ethnic origins born between 1914 and 1923 were interviewed about the effects of menopause. Some of the women originally came from Central Europe and had been imprisoned in concentration camps. The result was surprising: although on the one hand – as expected – the stresses from this time had had a greater impact on health, 29% of the previously imprisoned women were in good mental health – despite these traumatic experiences.

Based on this result, the salutogenic question arose as to why people remain healthy or manage to recover despite adverse and difficult circumstances. From this, Antonovsky derived the coherence model, which provides answers.

The term coherence means connection and consistency. According to Antonovsky, the sense of coherence is "…a global orientation that expresses the extent to which someone has a pervasive, enduring, yet dynamic sense of confidence, first, that the demands from the inner and outer worlds of experience over the course of life are structured, predictable, and explainable, and second, that the resources necessary to meet the demands are available. And third, that these demands are challenges worthy of investment and commitment." (Antonovsky, cited in Bengel and Lyssenko 2012, p. 16; translated by the author).

The sense of coherence is based on the following three components:

- Sense of comprehensibility: In Antonovsky's sense, this is understood to mean that people can cognitively process and evaluate events for themselves. In this way, an internal chain of logic is built up that supports the recognition of connections.
- Sense of manageability (feeling of being able to cope): As soon as there is a conviction or belief that demands can be met with one's own resources and competencies, this feeling is strengthened. Antonovsky also calls this instrumental confidence in one's own abilities.
- Sense of meaningfulness – the feeling of being in a meaningful place: From Antonovsky's point of view, this is the most important component, as it deals with the meaning of one's life: Is the energy and effort expended worth facing the problems and challenges? Or is there no corresponding motivation? Then life also seems neither meaningful nor significant.

Figure 2.1 shows a model of what the sense of coherence is based on.

In terms of resilience, the result of the study is extremely helpful, as it supports a cognitive approach that deals with the essential question of life: the question of meaning. The coherence model provides important clues when it comes to cognitively mastering crises and adverse circumstances.

In addition, a paradigm shift was initiated: From the pathological approach to an approach that understands health as a continuous process of coming to terms with the environment with the help of one's own resources. This basic idea also flows into resilience research: resilience is understood as a dynamic process that can be initiated preventively in order to acquire resources for possible crises.

In addition to this salutogenic concept, there are other scientific findings, especially from a neuroscientific perspective, that support the resilience concept. More on this in the next chapter.

Fig. 2.1 Coherence model.
(Source: Wikipedia https://
de.wikipedia.org/wiki/
Salutogenese accessed
08/11/2018)

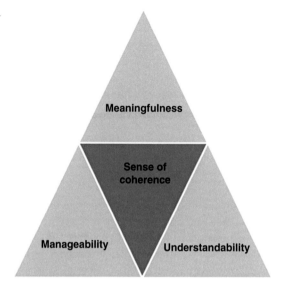

2.3   Supportive Neuroscientific Findings

In recent years, a number of neuroscientific findings have been made that support
the resilience theory and derived concepts and thus establish new connections and
make them understandable. From a neuroscientific point of view, resilience research often draws on previous findings in stress research, since the active processing and evaluation of stress triggers or stress factors is a key element of resilience.
In the following, selected findings are drawn on the following topics:

- Findings from stress research
- Findings on basic psychological needs
- Insights from towards and away-from reactions
- Insights into the valuation system and neuroplasticity

2.3.1 Findings from Stress Research

▶ What findings from stress research are helpful in better understanding resilience theory?

Stress research assumes that the triggers of stress, so-called stressors, are evaluated very individually. This means as an example that a stressor such as working in an open-plan office does not always have to lead to stress reactions. The principle applies here that stressors per se are not to be regarded as negative, but that it is the corresponding individual assessment that is decisive. Figure 2.2 shows the possible evaluation of a stressor.

In the event that the stressor triggers a negative evaluation and thus stress, the human body has developed natural processes and mechanisms to deal with the released hormone cocktail and process it accordingly in the body.

From a neuroscientific point of view, this way of processing (dangerous) stimuli is a biological legacy from earlier times, because the survival of humans in the wilderness was dependent on the speed of stimulus processing in the brain: i.e. the faster the reaction to danger, the higher the survival rate. This reaction is called the fight-or-flight response and describes the rapid physical adaptation to the situation. In this process, emotions help to immediately evaluate the dangerous situation on the basis of the stimuli.

▶ What does stimulus processing of stressors look like?

The processing of stimuli takes place in two stages: The primary stimulus processing takes place partly in the unconscious as a component of the limbic system: The amygdala "checks" within milliseconds whether something is threatening for the system. Only secondary stimulus processing allows stored information from previous experiences to be retrieved and the existing situation to be compared with

Fig. 2.2 Stressor and possible assessments. (Own representation)

it. This is done with the help of the hippocampus and (somewhat delayed) the pre-frontal cortex. At this point, a decision is made as to whether there is "danger" or "no danger". In case of "danger", automatic routines and reaction patterns are initi-ated that have the goal of preparing the body – for flight or fight. Among other things, the hypothalamus activates the sympathetic nervous system, which in turn initiates a cascade of hormone releases to ultimately affect the organs. For exam-ple, cortisol inhibits the immune system, suppresses inflammation, and supports the regeneration of glucose to have energy on hand in case of emergency. Increased blood pressure improves blood flow to the muscles, while inhibiting the energy supply to the stomach and reproductive organs.

From today's perspective, cortisol secretion supports human performance: in case of optimal arousal, this is helpful to be effective and productive. But in case of overexcitation, the thinking capacity of the prefrontal cortex – and thus conscious thinking – is inhibited, and proven and well-known reaction patterns, controlled from the brain stem, run automatically and control the body.

Whether stress is experienced as distress – negative stressors – or as eustress – positive stressors – is determined by one's own evaluation. The body has also de-veloped mechanisms to reduce and process the hormone cocktail with the help of the parasympathetic nervous system.

▶   What stress model supports these neuroscientific findings?

These neuroscientific findings are incorporated and extended in other models such as the transactional stress model according to Richard Lazarus, a common model for stress management. After filtering the stimuli, the stressors are subjectively evaluated, depending on context, previous experiences and physical condition. If the result of the primary assessment is "dangerous", a further secondary assessment takes place, depending on the resources available, leading to negative stress if re-sources are lacking, and appropriate coping strategies – these are discussed below – are deployed. Figure 2.3 shows a simplified representation of the stress model.

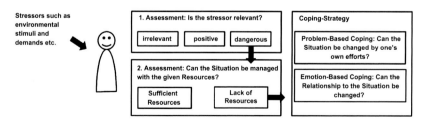

Fig. 2.3   Stress model according to Lazarus. (Cf. Struhs-Wehr 2017, p. 44 f)

At this point it may be emphasized that in the second assessment with sufficient resources eustress can occur and thus the stressor is positively assessed and in a broader sense also contributes to the build-up of resources. In case of a lack of resources, distress occurs and coping strategies become necessary. Coping strategies imply a positive way of dealing with stressors and are part of the concept of stress balance.

In general, two coping approaches are distinguished: Either the problem can be solved by one's own efforts or one's own attitude towards the problem can be changed. Both coping strategies support one's own learning process in dealing with stressors and thus promote resilience. From a neurological point of view, a cognitive re-evaluation takes place. This can take the following four forms (cf. Rock 2011, p. 172ff.):

- Re-interpretation: This means a conscious decision that an event originally classified as dangerous is no longer so.
- Normalization: With normalization, stressful situations are presented and perceived as "normal" and consequently accepted, for example, with the help of an explanation. This puts situations in relation to each other and puts them into perspective.
- Rearrangement of information: When re-evaluating circumstances, a lot of energy is needed to create new mental maps (using synaptic connections to create neuron patterns that can be retrieved). These in turn support the structuring and reconfiguration of new orders in the brain.
- Repositioning: This builds on the reorganization, which can be most effectively designed with the help of a change of perspective on oneself. In this way, a new position can be created.

All these different possibilities of reassessment support the process of stress balance or the original reaction to danger. This is accompanied by a dynamic process to train resilience – through cognitive reassessment.

In addition, there are other neuroscientific principles whose knowledge is conducive to resilience in a team.

2.3.2   Findings on Basic Psychological Needs

▶   What neuroscientific findings on basic needs are relevant to resilience
theory?

According to neuropsychotherapist Klaus Grawe, the human system strives for
consistency in its basic psychological needs in order to be healthy. The basis are
motivational schemata that people acquire consciously and unconsciously in the
course of development – based on experience gained in order to satisfy their needs.
Motivational schemas determine how we experience and perceive the environment
and can be expressed through an action of approach or avoidance. Here is an example: If the need for control and orientation can be well satisfied in external experience and behavior, since performed actions, such as a request to a colleague
that is granted – lead to the expected goal, this person experiences himself as self-
efficacious and supports the approach schema. These positive experiences of control contribute significantly to the formation of one's own self-esteem, which has a
positive effect on the human system level. With the formation of the human being,
different experiences are made which overlap and can no longer be assigned to
individual actions with regard to the goals. However, if a person does not experience himself as self-efficacious, because, for example, a basic need cannot be fulfilled, then patterns of behaviour arise from this, which repeatedly produce precisely this deficiency (cf. Grawe 2004, p. 208 f.).

In order for basic needs to be met safely, a deficiency in the sense of inconsistency must first be signalled at the human system level. According to the consistency principle, actions or incentives are derived from this to cover the needs.
Figure 2.4 shows a simplified representation of Grawe's consistency principle and
the basic psychological needs (cf. Grawe 2004, p. 189).

In the following, we will mainly explain the points of contact with resilience
theory that arise from basic needs and their satisfaction according to consistency.

Grawe assumes that people act in a goal-oriented manner in order to satisfy
their needs and that inconsistencies provide a boost for this. This is because
inconsistent states are avoided by systems. This requires specifications that are
fulfilled. If these are fulfilled in the sense of a positive control experience, self-
efficacy is promoted (Cf. Grawe 2004, p. 191). This allows the discovery and development of further flexible mechanisms for the satisfaction of needs. From a
neurological point of view, dopamine is released, and pathways are formed in the
brain that form mental maps (cf. Grawe 2004, p. 358).

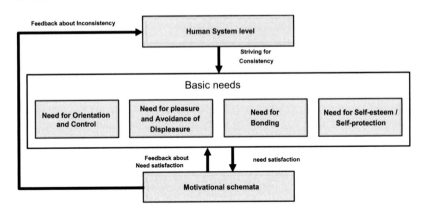

Fig. 2.4 Grawe's basic needs. (Cf. Grawe 2004, p. 189)

Constant experiences of inconsistency and a failure to meet needs, on the other hand, prevent the possibility of positive need satisfaction and limit the ability to "...cope positively with later stresses in life." (Grawe 2004, p. 192). Thus, these experiences have an impact on resilience. What exactly this can look like is exemplified by the basic need of attachment in the next section.

▶   What is the impact of the basic psychological need for bonding?

The need for bonding plays a major role when it comes to developing one's own self-efficacy. Research shows that people develop positively when this basic need is met positively in the sense of closeness and affection, even in babies. This has an impact on "...their self-confidence, their self-esteem, their self-efficacy expectations, their resilience (robustness) in the face of stress and, in particular, their interpersonal relationship behaviour and the quality of their relationships..." (Grawe 2004, p. 208). Neuroscientifically, this can also be seen as the hormone oxytocin is released. This makes us trusting, promotes social behavior and supports emotional regulation. For this reason, there are different mental maps for "enemies" or "friends" as different mental circuits are linked and headed for: The one for enemies provides an away-from response, the one for friends provides a toward response. The latter enhances the effect of mirror neurons, while the other suppresses mirror neurons, allowing for less compassion and empathy, which also automatically leads to an away-from reaction. In addition, positive relationships cause an increase in performance.

Insights from Towards and Away-From Reactions

According to Dr. Evian Gordon, "…all human actions…are based on the brain's determination to minimize danger and maximize reward." (Rock 2011, p. 143). This leads to the brain reviewing the stimuli it receives according to the very principles of danger avoidance and reward gaining and deciding accordingly. Along with this, it can be concluded that people tend to stay in the familiar and known comfort-zone in order not to adjust to the new and/or unknown, because this costs energy. The latter can also be saved if (thinking) routines are introduced.

The two principles of minimizing danger and maximizing reward lead to so-called toward or away-from reactions, with the limbic system mainly making these decisions. When towards responses succeed in people because, for example, they are curious about something or enjoy it, dopamine, a neurotransmitter, is released. It also supports and stabilizes the formation of mental maps.

Away-from reactions lead to increased cortisol levels in the blood, which activate vital functions. The more the away-from reaction decreases, the more the cortisol levels in the blood decrease.

2.3.3 Insights from Evaluation Systems and Neuroplasticity

▶   What makes the rating system of resilient people different from others?

It is known from Raffael Kalisch's elaborated PAS theory (Positive Appraisal Style) that the threat appraisal, i.e. the subjective appraisal of a situation is generally rated as rather positive by resilient people – compared to people who are non-resilient, so to speak. That is, resilient individuals generally evaluate stimuli and situations more positively than the realistic situation in reality is - in comparison with non-resilient individuals. Figure 2.5 shows Kalisch's representation, where the "0" stands for the realistic evaluation of situations (cf. Kalisch 2017, p. 135 f.).

The amazing thing is that this evaluation system adapts and "grows", so to speak, with the experience of crises and resistance, because the brain is neuroplastically predisposed. This ensures that new mental maps can develop in the brains right up till old age. With the help of mental maps, coherent information is stored in the brain, e.g. for movement sequences. This happens all the more easily if the new thing to be learned is enjoyed by the learner, as this stimulates the release of dopamine, which supports the formation of mental maps in the brain.

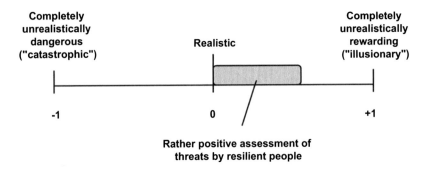

Fig. 2.5 Kalisch's representation of threat assessment by resilient people. (Cf. Kalisch 2017, p. 135)

The fact, that neuroplasticity promotes resilience in the presence of positive control experience is supported by the information that the stress and reward systems inhibit each other: In case where potential rewards are in prospect, the reward system is activated and at the same time the stress system is inhibited to perceive stressors. This could also lead to the conclusion that people who do not evaluate difficult situations as such also remain resilient. From a neuroscientific point of view, this perspective is supported. However, it has not yet been fully confirmed by studies.

These selected neuroscientific findings form a further basis for the following definition of resilience.

Definition of Resilience

3

> *Our greatest weakness lies in giving up. The sure way to success is always to try again.*
>
> Thomas Edison

Based on the studies and the insights gained from the above chapters, resilience is defined below – as far as the current state of science allows. As resilience research has only been considered a scientific discipline in its own for just under 20 years, further results from ongoing studies are still expected.

The word resilience comes from the English and means "elasticity and resistance". It was predominantly used to determine the condition of a material: If pressure was applied to a material and the material returned to its original shape after the period of pressure, then this material was called resilient.

Resilience has entered common parlance in the sense of "psychological resilience" or in the Duden dictionary as "...the ability to survive difficult life situations without sustained impairment..." (Duden "Resilienz" 2018). Implicit in these explanations is the assumption that there must first have been a risk, adversity or crisis situation that was overcome with the help of existing resources and skills in order to be resilient. In other words, resilience only becomes apparent in the process of coping, or in retrospect, and is not an innate ability. Resilience is also acquired in a domain-specific manner and can only be partially transferred from one area of life to another. Figure 3.1 shows the development process towards resilience.

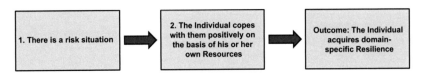

Fig. 3.1 Resilience development. (Own representation based on Fröhlich-Gildoff and Rönnau-Böse 2015, p. 10)

The concept of resilience is thus a dynamic, active process, as people can actively adapt to adversity. Crucial to resilience in this context is "…the maintenance or rapid restoration of mental health during and after adversity." (Kalisch 2017, p. 28). It is important to note that resilience is not only used in crises, but also plays an important role in natural development processes to promote one's self-efficacy. This is defined as a "…confidence in one's own abilities and available resources and the conviction that one can achieve a certain goal even by overcoming obstacles…" (Fröhlich-Gildoff and Rönnau-Böse 2015, p. 46). The development of self-efficacy is inherent in humans and can be acquired very early in life. Grawe even speaks of a basic need for orientation and control that every human being carries within him or herself (Cf. Grawe 2004, p. 230ff.). If this need is satisfied in the sense of a positive experience of control after an initiated action, then this leads to positive self-efficacy. This is not only about active actions that influence self-efficacy, but also about one's own expectations that are confirmed on a mental level. With this confirmation, neurotransmitters are again released in the brain, creating corresponding pathways as part of the mental maps in the brain. The development of this already begins in childhood.

▶   What are the positive consequences of resilience?

The following is a list of these:

- Resilience supports the necessary adaptation processes to master crises or adverse circumstances in different areas of life (e.g. physical, social, mental, and societal). Under certain circumstances, the resilience gained in one area can be transferred to another, thus making further options for action transparent.
- One's own resources are made aware and thus an understanding of how these are strengthened is also promoted. The principle of "strengthening strengths" applies.

- The acquired resilience supports not only in the various development processes, but also in dealing with everyday stressful situations. Due to increasing work density, this is an important aspect especially in the professional context.
- From the point of view of resilience research and the associated dissemination of results, stress-related illnesses can be reduced with the help of the application of the concept, and one's own self-efficacy can be increased due to an improved and conscious promotion of resources – on an individual and team level.

In the following chapter, team-relevant terms are briefly introduced and the understanding of resilience in a team is deepened.

Teamwork and Resilience in the Team

4

> *In order to be able to achieve something, everyone must consider their activity to be important and good.*
>
> Leo Tolstoy

Much has already been written about teams and their various compositions. Therefore, only a few essential aspects that are helpful in this context will be discussed here.

4.1   About Teams and Teamwork

Duden defines the term team as a "…group of people who work together on a task." (Duden 2018). In general, a team is a dynamic, productive, social system (Cf. Poggendorf, p. 28 f.): Team members are social beings who relate to each other and carry out interactions that aim at productive outcomes. The success and performance of a team often depends on how well the team uses internal group dynamics to accomplish a task. The basic idea of teamwork is that the interaction of all team members makes a result possible that each individual could not have been achieved on his or her own. Teamwork is the preferred method of working especially when complexity increases and employees are given the opportunity to "…have more creative freedom and opportunities to participate in their work." (Poggendorf, p. 30).

From a systemic point of view, the members of a team consistently see themselves as a social unit or element in an organizational system. In this context, the respective system and its elements belong to each other systemically and relate to each other: "Because in order to build an efficient team, you have to look at the individual, involve and qualify… (and) …in order to promote the individual efficiently, you need a qualified team." (Poggendorf, p. 22). Team development thus always takes place on two levels: the individual level and the team level. The process of team development is usually supported by a team coach or team developer and has the goal of building a functional, well-cooperating, high-performing team. It is helpful if there is consensus on the following aspects (cf. Poggendorf, p. 32):

- There is a common understanding of the set goal and the expected result.
- Team members recognize that the skills and competencies of individuals complement each other well within the team, contributing to something greater.
- Common team rules are established, that are enforced in terms of structure and communication, and where the team is also jointly responsible to fulfill those.
- There is a common understanding of leadership.
- The decision-making processes and decision-making competencies are transparent and are adhered to.

Due to the existing team dynamics, these aspects are always put to the test – and are usually evident in the form of group dynamic processes. Bruce Tuckman published the concept of the team clock in 1965 with the following four phases of team development:

- Forming (also called the foundation or orientation phase)
- Storming (also called conflict or melee phase)
- Norming (also called the organizing phase or the familiarity phase)
- Performing (also called the constructive cooperation phase)

In addition, there are other models of team dynamics, all of which have the aspect in common that their development processes are seldom linear, but usually proceed in waves. In the best case, an oscillation between the two poles of differentiation and integration can be observed, whereby differentiation is to be understood as discourse at this point. After a discourse, the next phase is the integration of what has been learned. This oscillation between differentiation and integration enables a development in the team. This is illustrated in Fig. 4.1, which shows the non-linear team process.

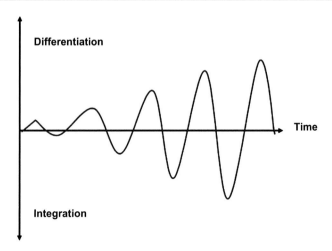

Fig. 4.1 Non-linear team process between the poles of differentiation and integration. (Cf. König and Schattenhofer 2006, p. 58)

With this development, the amplitudes can also become larger if the content leading to the differentiation phase is integrated again and again. In this way, the options for action for individuals and teams become larger and more diverse. If, on the other hand, teams only strive in one of the two directions, then there is a risk of "heat death" (Cf. König and Schattenhofer 2006, p. 58 f.), for example, during the integration phase – i.e. the team members act too homogeneously. On the other hand, if there is too much differentiation, there is a risk of offending conflicts, which can lead to dysfunctional teams and non-performing teamwork and ultimately to the dissolution of the team.

If team development and team performance do not proceed in a linear fashion, but rather in waves, how can resilience be promoted in the team in order to defy adverse circumstances? The following chapter provides insights into this.

4.2   Resilience in the Team

Having explained and introduced the concepts of resilience at a personal level, the question remains as to what these different approaches mean for teams. Usually, the goal is a high-performing team, whereby this is characterized by trusting interactions, transparent communication, clear structures and a strong commitment to completing tasks.

In general, some resilience approaches can be transferred from the "human system" to the "team system". Especially when it comes to stressful situations and resulting conflicts. The latter are precisely the adverse circumstances that then play an important role in the area of resilience in the team and can be overcome with the help of coping strategies.

▶   To what extent do team dynamic processes play a role within team resilience?

The resilience of a team is also a dynamic, active process, because depending on the nature of the adverse circumstances or crises and the application of coping strategies, development in a positive sense – combined with a promotion of resources – that of the individual and the team emerges. Figure 4.2 shows the team dynamic processes that allow development with the oscillation between the adverse circumstances and coping:

The graph supports the view that resilient teams are characterised by their ability to cope with adverse circumstances. The faster and better this coping succeeds, the more efficient teams are or remain. Moreover, successful teams have developed patterns and draw on their resources to cope with adverse circumstances. If, on the other hand, teams are not resilient, in the sense that they are unable to cope with adverse circumstances or crises, the consequences are conflicts and stressful behaviour in a negative sense – which has an impact on the level of the individual and the team.

▶   What other aspects from individual resilience can be applied to team resilience?

- As soon as a team experiences itself as self-effective, its own team experience becomes tangible in terms of success and performance. There are countless examples of this in team sports.
- The feeling of meaningfulness in the team is also answered by the question of whether the efforts and the energy invested in the teamwork are also worthwhile. It is advantageous that the sense of purpose can be initiated by one of the team members as well as from the outside—like the organisational purpose itself.
- If there are already resilient people in a team, this has an effect on the whole team: From a neurological point of view, mirror neurons support the perception of emotions and thus understanding in the team. It is known from Werner's studies that reference persons or role models for individuals support their own resilience.

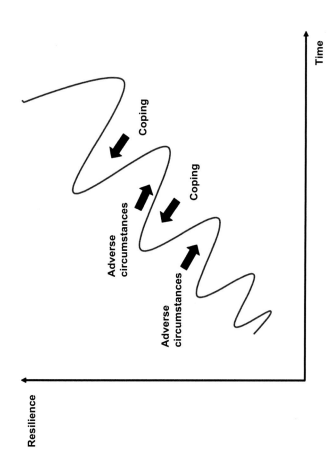

Fig. 4.2 Resilient team development based on the poles of adverse circumstances and application of coping strategy. (Own representation)

- Positive crisis management by individual team members also promotes resilience in the team, since the team and its members relate to each other systemically. This also applies vice versa: a crisis overcome by the team promotes the resilience of the individual. This leads to the conclusion that resilience can also be trained and acquired in a team.

In sum, a resilient team is the basis for successful teamwork in a rapidly changing environment. Topics such as the increase in speed, the density of work and the degree of digitalization in professional contexts increasingly lead to adverse or challenging circumstances that need to be managed in terms of resilience. The positive control experiences of the team members and their resources form the basis for building and maintaining resilience.

For this, the application of the different resilience factors is helpful to make resources transparent and conscious, and to apply them. The possibilities for this will be taken up in the next chapter.

Resilience Factors

5

Do you always want to ramble? See, the good is so near.
Only learn to grasp happiness, for happiness is always
there.

Johann Wolfgang von Goethe

Based on the concept of protective and risk factors from the long-term studies, resilience factors were identified that allow resilience to be promoted and trained.

In the corresponding long-term studies, protective and risk factors were identified: Protective factors increase a person's resilience in dealing with difficult situations, while risk factors burden or weaken them.

Protective factors support or protect people in dealing with adverse situations and are divided into the categories internal and external. Internal protective factors are based in the person themselves, such as personal characteristics, skills, or experience, while external protective factors are defined as "resilience-promoting circumstances that a person finds in their environment and can use for themselves…" (Amann 2015, p. 9). Table 5.1 shows an exemplary list of internal and external protective factors.

In addition, to protective factors, there are also risk factors – these are primarily understood as factors that hinder development and can be identified on the one hand from within the child as vulnerability factors (in the sense of psychological injuries in childhood and thus the opposite of resilience) or as stress factors from

Table 5.1 Internal and external protective factors. (Cf. Amann 2015, p. 9ff)

Inner protective factors	External protective factors
Personal characteristics such as how helpful or communicative a person is	**Positive role models,** such as teachers from childhood, who have shaped you positively
Inner attitudes and beliefs, such as how optimistically a person views one's own life situation.	**Stimulating learning environment** such as allowing people to try new things at work in order to learn
Talents and gifts, such as what talents a person has and how they nurture them	**Reliable reference persons,** such as close friends or colleagues, who support one or who can be asked for advice

the environment. The latter relate primarily to the current environment, for example in everyday working life. There are many examples of stress factors in the work environment, such as these:

- Finishing under deadline pressure
- Social isolation at work
- Constant availability
- Unfavourable working atmosphere among colleagues
- Etc.

The better a person balances the risk factors with the protective factors, the better they succeed in coping with the situation. This has given rise to the resilience factors in general, which differ depending on the book and author. In this book they are the following ones, which are further subdivided into "basic attitudes" and "aspects for action", whereby both are skills that can be learned. Figure 5.1 shows the eight resilience factors.

The resilience factors mentioned will be applied to individuals at this point, but will be transferred to the concerns of teams in the further course.

The resilience factors of the basic attitude include the following aspects:

- Optimism: With the basic attitude of optimism, people believe in the possibilities of a positive outcome of their actions. This also implies a confident attitude towards the future – especially despite adverse circumstances that may exist at the moment.
- Acceptance: People with this basic attitude accept the unchangeable – instead of beating themselves up about it – and concentrate on their own influencing factors – instead of on what lies outside their sphere of influence.

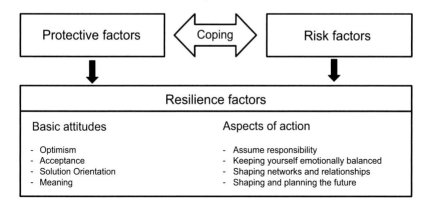

Fig. 5.1 Resilience factors. (Own representation)

- Solution orientation: With a solution-oriented basic attitude, people direct their attention to the possible and a solution space. In this way they become able to act again and promote different options for the future.
- Meaning: With a global orientation or a sense of coherence (according to Antonovsky) it is possible for people to give meaning to their own actions.

The resilience factors related to the aspects for action or learnable skills include the following:

- Taking responsibility: People who take responsibility for themselves and their actions put aside their victim role and use the available space and options for action.
- Keeping yourself emotionally balanced: Finding emotional balance again and again is an important step for everyone. Because this allows a "both/and" view, e.g. on the aspects of tension and relaxation, flexibility and structure – and this also on an emotional level.
- Shaping networks and relationships: People desire to be valued. This includes, among other things, cultivating appreciative relationships and giving and receiving support from others.
- Planning and shaping the future: People who set and pursue appropriate goals for the future calculate difficulties and work out alternative courses of action.

The principle of self-efficacy may be assumed for all resilience factors, in order to generally promote the formation of resources and one's own development – both for team members and within the team.

In the following, the various resilience factors are each taken up and extended to the concerns of teamwork. Possible models, guiding questions and intervention methods will be briefly outlined in order to deepen the knowledge about the resilience factors. These should be understood as initial suggestions on how resilience can be developed and promoted in teams.

5.1   Optimism

> To see clearly, it is often enough to change the direction of vision. (Antoine de Saint-Exupery).

▶   What concepts does the basic attitude of optimism include?

Key words: Optimistic view related to outcomes of action, flexibility, confidence, hope, a positive view of one-self and the world.

Optimism as a basic attitude of a team is one of the keys to success. This is because it goes hand in hand with the view of life that set expectations will be positively fulfilled. Let's take the example of a sports team: If they don't take the play-field optimistically, points will be given away simply because of this basic attitude. It is important to note that being optimistic is not the same as positive thinking, because the latter often ignores reality.

There are three main factors that promote an optimistic attitude (Cf. Horn and Seth 2013, p. 41 f.).

- Alternation of phases: Positive and negative phases alternate. The team's attitude is decisive, i.e. the attitude with which the team members approach the respective phases. This aspect also applies to the duration of stressful situations or crises: Resilient teams perceive negative phases as limited in time and not as something perpetual.
- Differentiation instead of generalization: Optimistic teams already differentiate in their communication when it comes to evaluations and, above all, mutual feedback.
- Attributions: Optimistic teams do not take failures personally and do not see themselves as victims of circumstances. Successes are attributed to their own competence, performance, and thus self-efficacy.

In the aforementioned resilience theory according to Kalisch, a rather positive evaluation style is also attributed to resilient people. This also has an effect on resilient teams.

▶ Which guiding questions are helpful?

- How positive is the team about accomplishing the common task?
- How confident is the team that it can perform the common task under the given circumstances? What would be necessary to increase or compromise safety?
- In general, how are possible outcomes to team decisions and agreed actions evaluated?
- How confident are individual team members about the future?
- How do we inspire each other to enjoy getting the work done?

▶ Which model supports the understanding of the basic attitude of optimism?

Teamwork and cohesion between the team members often runs in waves in performing teams. That is, there are phases in which the teamwork works very well and the team feels connected to each other and phases in which the team moves apart or lives apart. When team dynamics are managed well, teams perform well and have the chance to develop. In Fig. 5.2, a representation is chosen in which the phases of low and high team cohesion are put in relation to each other. When team cohesion is low, team performance is usually correspondingly low.

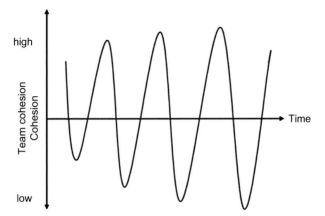

Fig. 5.2 Team cohesion within the team. (Own representation)

On the basis of this representation, the work of integration is perceived as something necessary, simply by the fact that the curve swings downwards. But what if these phases of cohesion and integration were simply represented differently on the axes? Figure 5.3 gives one way to illustrate this.

With the help of this representation, the view of the opposing development process and its cycles changes, because they are thus recognized as equal and complementary.

Optimistic teams perceive differentiation and the associated exchange and discourse as enriching, because they know about the importance of these phases.

▶   Which interventions are conducive to the basic attitude of optimism in
     the team?

A. Team boards: In some companies that already promote the agile way of working, positive things such as progress in projects or similar are communicated transparently to everyone in the team via public team boards. This makes it possible to repeatedly reflect on the jointly achieved goals and to acknowledge them.

Fig. 5.3 Team cohesion in a team – in a tilted representation. (Own representation)

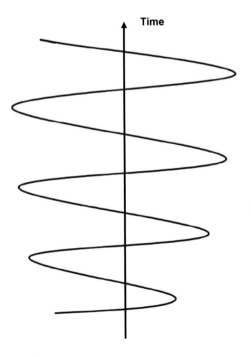

B. Seeing the good in the bad: From a systemic point of view, this intervention is especially helpful in difficult situations, as it supports the change of perspective and thus creates solution spaces. The questions go in the following direction: "Even if we evaluate it as negative at the moment – for what is what happened good – at the moment? Or also for the future in a few months? What can we learn from it?

C. Appreciative Inquiry: The concept explores positive circumstances in various phases and thus promotes shared resources and positive interaction within the team. Here, too, the principle applies that strengthening one's own "strengths" contributes much more to further development than focusing on weaknesses.

5.2 Acceptance

There is no way to happiness. Happiness is the way (Buddha).

▶ What concepts does the basic attitude of acceptance include?

Key words: Accepting changes and also the unchangeable, understanding and accepting crises and problems as opportunities, openness, calmness, mindfulness.

Usually, the brain is focusing on minimizing danger. In today's (working) environment, this is expressed by an increased focus on (possible) problems. However, this ignores what is really happening in this current moment or in the now. Approaches from the field of meditation and mindfulness help to positively influence brain structures (e.g., through regular meditation and the application of mindful methods) and to experience serenity and mindfulness in teamwork (cf. Haas 2015, p. 93 f.). Furthermore, the methods from mindfulness, such as the MBSR (Mindful Based Stress Reduction) program, support the basic attitude of acceptance. Countless studies have neurologically proven the positive effectiveness.

▶ Which guiding questions are helpful?

- How are unchangeable framework conditions dealt with in the team? Are these constantly questioned, and do they consume energy? Or can they be integrated well?
- How mindful are we of each other as a team? How present is each individual in this moment of encounter?
- What can the team itself influence? What indirectly? And what not at all – and consequently needs to be accepted?

- To what extent is there a demarcation with regard to one's own sphere of influence within the team? And outside the team?
- Are generally emotions named and dealt with empathetically?

▶   Which model supports the understanding of the basic attitude of acceptance?

In change processes, the model of the change curve according to Elisabeth Kübler-Ross is applied. In the 1960s, she interviewed more than 200 people in the USA who were told that they were terminally ill. In her questioning, she focused purely on the emotions and feelings that emerge and are experienced by the individuals and was thus able to identify a pattern consisting of five different phases, not always occurring in succession. These are: Denial, Anger, Bargaining, Depression, and Acceptance. After publication, researchers have successfully transferred and applied the "Five Stages of Grief" model to other areas of life where major changes have occurred such as loss of loved ones, layoffs, etc. This has helped to better explain the different emotional stages. Enclosed is a brief explanation of the five phases:

- Denial – is the first reaction. People do not want to acknowledge the change or believe that there is a confusion and that they are not the addressees of the change.
- Anger – as soon as people realize that the denial of the situation can no longer continue, they are frustrated and become angry. Often this phase is accompanied by the question "Why me?", "How can this happen only to me?" and "Who is guilty?".
- Bargaining – in this phase people hope and negotiate about the given circumstances and vow to improve.
- Depression – the communicated message becomes a reality and people fall into a depressed mood.
- Acceptance – in this phase, people begin to accept the situation and submit to the circumstances, so to speak. This is also accompanied by stabilization of the emotional roller coaster and emotions.

Figure 5.4 shows the change curve according to Kübler-Ross.

The change curve is helpful when it comes to tracking one's own reactions and perceived self-efficacy to change. This supports the acceptance of emotions – by oneself and by other team members.

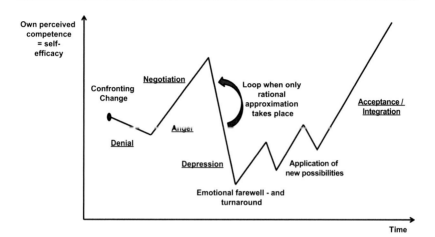

Fig. 5.4 Change curve according to Kübler-Ross. (https://www.cleverism.com/ understanding-kubler-ross-change-curve/. Accessed on 13.11.2018 with German translation by the author)

▶   Which interventions are conducive to the basic attitude of acceptance
       in the team?

A. Normalize or put into relation: Normalizing means comparing a current situation with another situation that is considered "normal" and thus socially accepted. This usually results in a relativization of the current situation. This also applies to the application of the change curve and its phases.

B. Seeing the good in the bad (see above): This intervention is also conducive to the basic attitude of acceptance.

C. Reassessment: Reassessment, as described above, also supports the change of perspective and thus allows the possibility of acceptance.

5.3   Solution Orientation

Don't look for mistakes, look for solutions (Henry Ford).

▶   Which terms does the basic attitude of solution orientation include?

Key words: Flexibility, letting go, awareness of the present, change of perspective, options for action, moving away from problem orientation.

Table 5.2 Problem and solution orientation

In problem orientation, it is important to…	In the solution orientation, it is important to…
Investigate the problem, Know the reason for the problem, Understand the problem and Use this information to address the problem	Identify solutions or parts of solutions, Identify resources that contribute to the solution, Progress, Be pragmatic, and to work out the solution

Table 5.3 Question directions

Problem-oriented lines of questioning ask…	Solution-focused questioning directions ask…
Problems	Opportunities
Causes	Exceptions
Debt	Conditions for success
Failure	Solutions
Error	Resources
Resistors	Talents
Risks	Contributions to the solution
Past	First, small steps
Improvement	Future
Why	What for

A solution-oriented attitude in teams is particularly noticeable in communication styles when solution-oriented questions are preferred to problem-oriented ones and are applied. Table 5.2 shows a distinction between problem and solution orientation.

For a better understanding, please find enclosed a further orientation with regard to the question directions in Table 5.3.

These lines of questioning are taken up again in the guiding questions.

▶   Which guiding questions are helpful?

- What is the focus of attention? On the problem or increasingly on the solution?
- Is there a willingness to solve the problem and let go? Or is the current benefit from the problem greater than the solution sought?
- How do we become or remain capable of acting as a team?
- Does everyone have the same understanding of the problem and its current implications? Are there differences in perception?

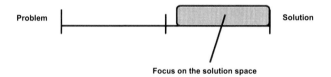

Fig. 5.5 Focus on solution space. (Own representation)

▶   Which model supports the understanding of the basic attitude of solu-
    tion orientation?

With the help of the questions already mentioned, the focus can be put on the
solution space. This leaves teams with the responsibility and power to enable new
thinking. Figure 5.5 shows a sketch of how this can be modelled.

▶   Which interventions are conducive to the basic attitude of solution
    orientation in the team?

A. Miracle question: This is used when the team shows the first willingness to
accept solutions after a crisis. The team is asked to imagine a hypothetical future in
which everything is allowed and there are no more problems – like when a miracle
happened. This imagination is deepened with the views of everyone in the team or
with the help of a description of a daily routine. This opens up new perspectives
that were previously only imaginable to a limited extent, and addresses solution
spaces.
    B. Resources from the past with the team timeline: A team timeline is often used
to reflect on events from the commonly shared history. The focus can be placed on
problems that have been overcome and the strengths that have been gained by
doing so. In this way, common team resources are made transparent that are helpful
for solution orientation.
    C. Change of perspective: The change of perspective on a problem is helpful to
create possible solution spaces.

5.4   Meaning

Those who plant trees even though they know they will never sit in their shade have
at least begun to understand the meaning of life (Rabindranath Thakur).

▶   What concepts does the basic attitude of sense-making include?

Key words: Meaningfulness, values, cohesion, significance, global orientation, trust, worthwhile use of resources.

According to a study by Tatjana Schnell, four components play a role in making work seem meaningful (Cf. Schnell 2018, p. 32 f.):

1. Coherence – this means that the content tasks fit the skills and the circumstances.
2. Significance – this means that the contribution made is taken seriously.
3. Orientation – this means that the strategy and orientation of the company is in line with its own values.
4. Belonging – this means that people can identify with the company and thus feel they belong to something bigger.

These components can also be applied to teams and their joint collaboration.

According to Antonovsky, meaningfulness arises when it is related to everyday activities and when overcoming everyday challenges is also rewarded by one's own commitment the effort made.

▶ Which guiding questions are helpful?

- To what greater good do we as a team meaningfully contribute with our collective teamwork?
- What does each individual on the team contribute to? What can the team trust in each individual? What am I – in return – willing to give?
- What values and vision support us in what we do?
- Who creates meaning? And what for?

▶ Which model supports the understanding of the basic attitude of meaning?

Antonovsky's coherence model described above is based on the questions of meaningfulness and the two components of manageability and comprehensibility. Only when these are also answered at the team level is a global orientation and trust given.

▶ Which interventions are conducive to the basic attitude of sense in the team?

A. Reflection questions: answering the reflection questions is primarily for learning and gathering insights. Examples include: Who provides meaning in our team? What values and actions does it support? How can meaning be further promoted?

B. Storytelling: With the help of storytelling, one's own motives, emotions and ways of thinking can be conveyed well. By extension, stories can also be meaningful as they touch the audience on a mental and emotional level. The guiding question of the team intervention might be, "What do I value being a member of this team…" This will foster more resources in the team and secure them with the help of the stories.

5.5   Taking Responsibility

> One is responsible not only for what one does, but also for what one does not do (Lao Tzu).

▶   What terms does the action aspect of taking responsibility include?

Key words: Putting aside the role of victim, standing up for oneself in the team, standing up for the team, taking personal responsibility and demanding it from others, setting boundaries, allowing help to oneself and others.

Taking responsibility for one's own actions is an essential component of resilience – especially when applied to teams. This resilience factor manifests itself in two ways: the personal responsibility that each person has towards themselves and the responsibility towards the team. The latter ensures the necessary commitment to achieve the common goals.

▶   Which guiding questions are helpful?

- What does responsibility mean for each individual? How is this evident?
- How can responsibility be assumed in a team?
- What responsibilities can be assumed by the team and individual team members?
- What room for maneuver needs to be exploited? For each individual and for the team?

▶   Which models support the understanding of the aspect of taking responsibility?

The first model for taking ownership of responsibility is the drama triangle from transactional analysis, which explains basic relationship patterns in a simplified form. In communication patterns, persons assume one of the following three roles and communicate accordingly in the role of victim, persecutor and/or rescuer – in case they do not take over responsibility for themselves. It is important to note, that none of the roles is better or worse valued than the other. Although at first it may seem that the rescuer may be a more positive role. However, even a rescuer, in order to be a rescuer, first requires a victim. If everyone takes responsibility for their own thoughts and actions, no rescuers are needed.

The drama triangle applies on two different levels:

- The first level concerns the preferred role that is taken on the one hand in interpersonal relationships and on the other hand in the inner dialogues with oneself. Inner dialogues are also a kind of mental map that are applied to oneself.
- The second level concerns the current dialogue in the team: rapid changes can take place between the three roles and each person can take on any role (sometimes unconsciously). I.e., within a dialogue, a person can go from the rescuer to the victim and back again to the role of the rescuer.

Likewise, the roles can also be transferred to team level or organizations: For example, the marketing department can act as a perpetrator towards the sales department and vice versa – with the focus on saving the customer with their products or services.

A solution from the drama triangle is usually accompanied by accepting the responsibility – and this is equally true when it comes to one's own (self-)responsibility. Figure 5.6 shows a pictorial representation of the drama triangle.

Fig. 5.6 Drama triangle. (Source Wikipedia: https://de.wikipedia.org/wiki/Dramadreieck. Accessed on 02.10.2018 with own adaptation: instead of pursuer, perpetrator was used)

Fig. 5.7 Circle-of-influence model in teams. (Cf. Covey 2006)

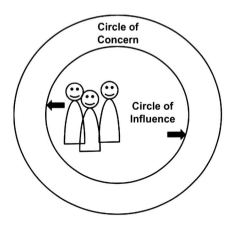

In addition, to the drama triangle, there is another model available: the Circle of Influence according to Stephen Covey. This helps to distinguish which topics can be influenced by the team – these are in the Circle of Influence – and which are not (these are therefore outside and the area is called Circle of Concern). Figure 5.7 shows the corresponding model.

Concern refers to things or issues that affect and concern the team but cannot be influenced by the team. In particular, a shared view of what lies within one's own sphere of influence and thus also within one's own responsibility is particularly conducive to the transparency and effectiveness of teamwork. In addition, there is the possibility of expanding one's own sphere of influence.

▶   Which interventions are conducive to the aspect of taking responsibility in the team?

A. Change of perspective: There are different types of change of perspective, at this point a form is chosen in which the perspective of a "team critic" and a "praise speaker" on the team performance is taken: Their perspectives can be elaborated and collected in a first step and reflected upon and possible actions derived in a second step. The change of perspective supports especially the integration work.

B. Team charter: A team charter is a document in which team agreements are jointly defined and thus provides orientation. Various aspects can be defined in terms of content, here is a selection:

• Establish the purpose of teamwork,
• Name team members,

- the principles on which action is taken,
- define the objectives and expected results,
- define the responsibilities within the team,
- define the measurement of results,
- design and define the decision-making processes.

Usually, a team charter is created at the beginning of a team composition and revised in defined intervals.

5.6   Keeping Yourself Emotionally in Balance

It is not what we experience, but how we feel about what we experience that makes up our fate (Marie von Ebner-Eschenbach).

▶   What concepts does the action aspect of keeping oneself emotionally
         in balance include?

Key words: Dealing with stress, tensions and relaxation in the team, naming one's own emotions, keeping energetic balance, dealing with conflicts.

The emotional balance in the team is an important factor in order to be able to perform. This raises the question of how emotions and stress are generally handled in the team – both the positive (eustress) and the negative (distress) ones. Because remaining in one of the extremes is not conducive: in both cases, recovery phases are necessary in order to regenerate.

From a neurological point of view, it is already advantageous to name and express one's own feelings – and not to suppress them. In addition, the naming of feelings already regulates emotions and promotes transparency and openness in the team.

For a successful regulation, which is understood at this point as a balance produce, the realizations from the Lazarus model are helpful to the stress regulation or also in the following to the optimal performance zone.

▶   Which guiding questions are helpful?

- What does emotional balance feel like in a team? What do we use to determine this? How can we achieve emotional balance?
- How do we deal with pressure, tension or stress in the team? How do we deal with relaxation?

- Can we structure the work in the team in such a way that we are and remain efficient?
- How can we communicate about emotions in an appreciative way? Do we name our feelings?

▶   Which model supports the understanding of the action aspect of keeping oneself emotionally in balance?

The optimal performance zone is a well-known model from the field of sports that provides information on emotional regulation. High performance in a team is only possible if there is an exact balance between tension and relaxation. Figure 5.8 shows the different zones and how they are characterized.

In order to experience high performance in a team, it is important to develop an understanding of which actions are helpful to target and maintain the optimal performance zone. For this purpose, the following techniques are helpful, e.g. to conduct a joint workshop in the team:

- Creating a common mood for the start
- Create Living rituals, e.g. looking back on what has already been done as part of a retrospective
- Identify and establish routines, e.g. a similar agenda structure.
- selectively hide minor disturbances that are distracting
- Being present in the room
- Set up routines
- Etc.

The experience of individuals can be transferred to the team.

▶   Which interventions are conducive to the aspect of keeping oneself emotionally in balance in the team?

A. Routines in everyday life: If routines are consciously established, they help to save energy. Routines can be established on two levels:

- at work level in the interaction between team members, as there is clarity and transparency,
- on a neurological level in the brain, as this leaves more energy for the prefrontal cortex.

An example of this can be that in joint team meetings a recurring structure of the process is followed with corresponding guiding questions.

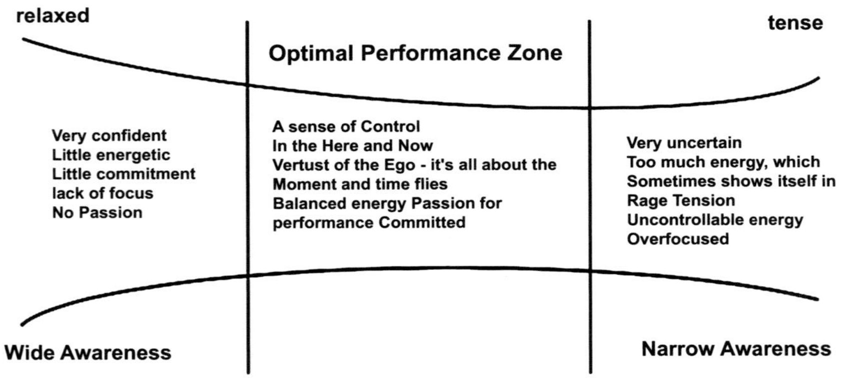

relaxed   **Optimal Performance Zone**   **tense**

Very confident
Little energetic
Little commitment
lack of focus
No Passion

A sense of Control
In the Here and Now
Vertust of the Ego - it's all about the
Moment and time flies
Balanced energy Passion for
performance Committed

Very uncertain
Too much energy, which
Sometimes shows itself in
Rage Tension
Uncontrollable energy
Overfocused

Wide Awareness   **Narrow Awareness**

Fig. 5.8 Optimal performance zone. (Cf. Center of Sports and Minds, accessed 04/20/2015, translated and adapted by author)

B. Stress balance: With the help of the optimal performance zone model, various goals and aspects can be discussed and measures derived. The first step is to identify the existing stressors. These can be of the following types:

- Physical stressors: These include heat, cold or noise in the office.
- Mental stressors: These arise in connection with performance requirements, such as constant time pressure, the feeling of being overtaxed or a high level of responsibility.
- Social stressors: Social stressors are demands that arise in interpersonal contact, such as unresolved, simmering conflicts, competitive situations, tensions.

C. Aspects of non-violent communication: Non-violent communication according to Marshall B. Rosenberg is more than a communication concept: it is about developing an attitude. This also involves communicating feelings and needs.

5.7   Shaping Networks and Relationships

Give and take, a law of all development (Christian Morgenstern).

▶   Which concepts are included in the action aspect of networking and shaping relationships?

Key words: Promote trust (culture), communicate within the team, promote team spirit, respect diversity, being in contact, meet at eye level, resolve conflicts.

Our lives are defined by relationships – starting with our first breath. This resilience factor is therefore of particular importance in the team environment. The selection of models and references is correspondingly large.

At this point, the aspect of the culture of trust is discussed, which effectively promotes performance in the team: "Because trust among colleagues releases substances (author's note: oxytocin) in the brain that lead to higher performance and better cooperation." (Zak 2017, p. 74). For this, it is helpful to give recognition and feedback. In the latter, feedback from relationships gives important clues about ourselves regarding our own self-efficacy. This promotes development: for the individual as well as in the whole team.

▶   Which guiding questions are helpful?

- How actively do we shape our relationships within the team? And outside with the stakeholders?
- How transparent do we make our communication – and thus also our relationship with each other?
- Which relationships are energetically balanced?
- What support can I expect and also give in the team?
- How do we deal with conflicts?
- Do we encourage and challenge each other as a team on the path to high performance?
- To which network does each team member have access?
- How is the network maintained and developed?
- Are we connected and able to give each other feedback?

▶   Which model supports the understanding of the aspect of action Shaping networks and relationships?

At this point, the Riemann-Thomann model is presented in excerpts. Fritz Riemann describes in his book "Basic Forms of Anxiety" that fears are the drivers for actions and has developed corresponding personality types. Christoph Riemann has further developed this model by naming wants and needs instead of fears. At this point, two basic fears and their desires are mentioned:

- The fear of not being able to develop as an individual leads to a schizoid personality type, which favors thinking over feeling in its judgmental function and has a desire to distance itself from others.
- The fear of not belonging leads to a depressive personality type, which favors feeling over thinking in its judgmental function and has a desire for closeness to others.

Figure 5.9 shows the poles of proximity and distance and their further distinguishing criteria.

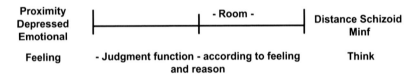

Fig. 5.9 Riemann-Thomann model in extracts. (Own representation according to Riemann 1961)

Due to the developed patterns and imprints, every person has a preference regarding the desire for closeness and distance. The knowledge of this supports how relationships can be shaped accordingly: more oriented towards closeness or towards distance.

►   Which interventions are conducive to the aspect of action Shaping networks and relationships in the team?

A. Team Constellations: The intervention of team constellations, in which team members position themselves in the room on various issues, is a very effective one. This allows transparency to be created very quickly as to how the individual team members position themselves on the topics. The questions can vary from simple to complex. The Riemann-Thomann model can also be used for constellations work.

B. Collegial case consultation: In collegial case consultation, it is possible for individual problem cases to be brought in and for the team colleagues to give feedback on them or share experiences and share this with the team. In this way, the wealth of experience of all is shared in the sense of resources.

In addition, many other interventions are possible and helpful – especially when it comes to conflicts within the team.

5.8   Planning and Shaping the Future

Courage is at the beginning of action, happiness at the end (Democritus).

►   What terms does the action aspect of planning and shaping the future include?

Key words: Define and pursue goals, actively plan the future, create vision, use imagination and willpower.

In order to plan and actively shape a future, goals are needed. These goals are best formulated as "towards" goals (instead of "away from" goals) together in the team. They include the following aspects, as they promote willpower (cf. Haas 2015, p. 70ff.):

Significance	The goal generates an inner positive resonance in all team members and thus a willpower that supports the achievement of the goal.
Own strengths	The strengths in the team and their team members are in line with the goals. If there are still strengths missing in the team that are needed, these can be acquired in the future.
Joy	The associated actions in the team generate joy. This is accompanied by a release of dopamine and an increase in performance.

The design component of the action aspect answers the "how?" question, e.g., "How can the formulated goal be implemented in the best possible way?"

▶   Which guiding questions are helpful?

• What does the future hold for us on the team? Next year? In 3 years? In 5 years?
• What goals do we want to set ourselves as a team? Which intermediate goals are sensible?
• What are our goals? How do we want to achieve them? What does appropriate planning and prioritization look like?
• Do the goals generate a positive response in terms of meaningfulness?

▶   Which model supports the understanding of the action aspect of planning and shaping the future?

According to the mountaineer's rule, which says: "Never look at the summit, but always look at the next steps", it is helpful under the overall goal to introduce intermediate goals: On the one hand, this makes the field smaller and more manageable, and on the other hand, it is more likely to contribute to a positive control experience as a consequence. The model of the target mountain is shown in Fig. 5.10 and includes metaphorical intermediate stages.

The Circle of Influence model is also helpful in shaping the future, as it supports clarity about influence.

Fig. 5.10 Target mountain
and intermediate stages.
(Own representation)

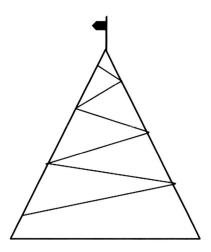

▶   Which interventions are conducive to the action aspect of shaping and
      planning the future in the team?

A. Strength-importance-joy: The team can relate its own strengths, importance
and joy to the formulated team goal: This provides the opportunity to identify further beneficial and obstructive aspects and to work on these accordingly.

B. Plan B: This intervention uses scenario work. This means that if a certain
path is planned for the achievement of the goal, a second path – a plan B – is
additionally created in order to be sure that the goal will also be achieved if plan A
does not take effect.

Example of Process Support to Promote Resilience in the Team

6

Focus all your energy not on fighting the old, but on creating the new.

Socrates

The greater the shared awareness of existing resources, the better the resilience in the team. The following agenda outlines a possible approach for process support using a workshop concept to promote knowledge of resilience factors and their implementation in everyday (team-) life. The following assumptions apply: There is a team that is not newly assembled but already has a shared history, and a facilitator accompanies the process. Figure 6.1 shows a proposed agenda including the required time slots. However, breaks are not included.

For a better understanding, the individual agenda points are taken up and explained:

Agenda Item: Check-in and Introduction to the Topic of Resilience
After the welcome, the participants are informed about the goal of the workshop: To strengthen resilience in the team and to raise awareness of resources conducive to this. Afterwards, the following guiding questions are answered by the team members:

- How am I doing - right now?
- If you were to describe resilience with a metaphor, what would it be?
- What aspect from resilience does this bring to bear?

© The Author(s), under exclusive license to Springer Fachmedien
Wiesbaden GmbH, part of Springer Nature 2023
M. Huber, *Resilience In The Team*, essentials,
https://doi.org/10.1007/978-3-658-39782-1_6

Agenda

- Check-in and introduction to the topic of resilience.
- Resilience theory and resilience factors - approx. 30 min.
- Team biography: Which difficult or challenging situations have we already mastered in the team? - approx. 60 min.
- Resilience factors in the team: Which resilience factors have been strengthened with what has been experienced? - approx. 60 min.
- Transfer: Which resilience factors do we want to promote with which concrete actions or anchor them in everyday life? - approx. 60 min.
- Conclusion and feedback - approx. 30 min.

Fig. 6.1 Agenda Team workshop on resilience. (Own representation)

The facilitator takes notes or sketches the metaphors openly on a flipchart.

Agenda Item: Resilience Theory and Resilience Factors
This agenda item provides information on resilience theory, e.g. on the basis of studies and the various resilience factors. It is helpful to present the information graphically.

Agenda Item: Team Biography: Which Difficult or Challenging Situations Have We Already Mastered in the Team?
With the help of the team biography, difficult or challenging situations can be viewed from the history. For this purpose, a timeline is drawn and the corresponding situations are marked. It is helpful to also question what has been learned in the various events – in the sense of a collection of resources and the transparency of the experienced self-efficacy.

The team biography also allows, on the one hand, an appreciation of what has already been achieved and, on the other hand, a better understanding and connection within the team.

Agenda Item: Resilience Factors in the Team: Which Resilience Factors Have Been Strengthened with the Experience?
The next step is to revisit the various events in the team through the lens of resilience factors. Possible guiding questions are:

- Which of the resilience factors are more prevalent in the team?
- Which of the resilience factors do we want to pay more attention to?

The result of the discussion of the guiding questions flows into the transfer.

Agenda Item: Transfer: Which Resilience Factors Do We Want to Promote with Which Concrete Actions or Anchor More in Everyday Life?
Concrete measures are defined that the team would like to implement. Instead of measures, team rules can also be derived in the cooperation, which the team agrees on in a binding manner. One example of this is not to question decisions once they have been made, but to accept and implement them in the sense of the resilience factor acceptance.

Another option is that each team member takes a personal measure in terms of the resilience factors and implements it from the day after.

Agenda Item: Conclusion and Feedback
At the end of the workshop, participants are asked to give their feedback and answer the question of how they are doing now.

The concept can be expanded or adapted accordingly. For example, if the team has just been appointed as such, personal stories can be introduced in which a difficult situation has been mastered. This increases the chance that the team members get to know each other better.

What You Can Take Away from This *Essential*

- Profound Basis for the Resilience Concept
- Background on building resilience in individuals and teams
- Ideas for implementing and promoting resilience in the team

M. Huber, *Resilience In The Team*, essentials,
https://doi.org/10.1007/978-3-658-39782-1

References

Amann, E.: Resilienz. Haufe, Freiburg (2015)

Bengel, J.: Was erhält Menschen gesund? Antonovskys Modell der Salutogenese – Diskussionsstand und Stellenwert; eine Expertise. In: Forschung und Praxis der Gesundheitsförderung. Bundeszentrale für gesundheitliche Aufklärung (BZgA). Köln. (2001)

Bengel, J., Lyssenko, L.: Resilienz und psychologische Schutzfaktoren im Erwachsenenalter – Stand der Forschung zu psychologischen Schutzfaktoren von Gesundheit im Erwachsenenalter. In: Forschung und Praxis der Gesundheitsförderung, Bd. 43. Bundeszentrale für gesundheitliche Aufklärung (BZgA), Köln (2012)

Center of Sports and Minds. http://www.centerforsportsandmind.com. Accessed: 20. Apr. 2015

Covey, S.: Die 7 Wege der Effektivität, Prinzipien für persönlichen und beruflichen Erfolg, ungekürztes Hörbuch erschienen am 3. Gabal Audio, Offenbach (Nov. 2006)

Duden „Resilienz": https://www.duden.de/suchen/dudenonline/resilienz. Accessed: 26. Sept. 2018

Fröhlich-Gildoff, K., Rönnau-Böse, M.: Resilienz. Reinhardt, München (2015)

Grawe, K.: Neuropsychotherapie. Hogrefe, Göttingen (2004)

Haas, O.: Corporate Happiness Als Führungssystem. Glückliche Menschen leisten gerne mehr. Schmidt, Berlin (2015)

Horn, S., Seth, M.: Stressfrei, gerne und erfolgreich arbeiten – Resilienz im Beruf. Herder, Freiburg im Breisgau (2013)

Kalisch, R.: Der resiliente Mensch: Wie wir Krisen erleben und bewältigen. Neueste Erkenntnisse aus Hirnforschung und Psychologie. Piper, München (2017)

König, O., Schattenhofer, K.: Einführung in die Gruppendynamik. Carl-Auer, Heidelberg (2006)

Poggendorf, A.: Angewandte Teamdynamik, Methodik für Trainer, Berater. Pädagogen und Teamentwickler. Cornelsen, Berlin (2012)

Rampe, M.: Der R-Faktor – Das Geheimnis Unserer Inneren Stärke. Frankfurt a. M, Eichborn (2004)

Riemann, F.: Grundformen der Angst. Reinhardt, München (1961)

Rock, D.: Brain at Work – Intelligenter arbeiten, mehr erreichen. Campus, Frankfurt (2011)

Schnell, T.: Man muss nicht gleich die Welt retten. Harvard Business Manager, Ausgabe Januar 2018, S. 32–35, Hamburg (2018)

Struhs-Wehr, K.: Betriebliches Gesundheitsmanagement und Führung – Gesundheitsorientierte Führung als Erfolgsfaktor im BGM. Springer, Heidelberg (2017)

Zak, P.: Wie Vertrauen die Leistung steigert. Harvard Business Manager, Ausgabe Mai 2017, S. 72–79, Hamburg (2017)

Printed in the United States
by Baker & Taylor Publisher Services